Requiem for David

Requiem for David

poems

Patrick T. Reardon

SILVER BIRCH PRESS
LOS ANGELES, CALIFORNIA

ISBN-13: 978-0997797251

EMAIL: silver@silverbirchpress.com

WEB: silverbirchpress.com

BLOG: silverbirchpress.wordpress.com

MAILING ADDRESS:
Silver Birch Press
P.O. Box 29458
Los Angeles, CA 90029

ACKNOWLEDGMENTS: Some poetry in this collection has appeared in the online magazine *Silver Birch Press* and in *Westigan Review.*

COVER: David Reardon, age four, April 1955.

Dedicated to Sarah, Tara, David
and, as always,
Cathy

In memory of David Reardon

With thanks to Thomas Pace, Patricia Cloud, Joan Servatius, and Julie Coplon. Special thanks to Melanie Villines.

Contents

Requiem for David

De Profundis

A Canticle for Pat

Requiem for David

BOTTOM TO TOP: David, Pat, Mom (1951)

1951 . . . foreign

She had no
language for
us. Felt our
foreign rhythms
like forest drums
under the skin, a
snake to break
through, tearing
tissue and turning
on her from
within. She
could not
abide the
chaos we
were. We
only felt lost.

LEFT TO RIGHT: David and Pat (1951)

1951 . . . abandon

Why did they take this photograph? David
is crying with loud abandon, and I stand there,
staring, fearful, uncertain, already on my way
to another place where I go deep to reach when
life squeezes too tight, as it often does.

I should have hugged David and consoled him. I
should be in this moment his big brother instead
of running away. I am gone, even as I stand there
and even as David cries with loud abandon, protesting
as he will through his life, angry and filled with
confusion and loss and not knowing how to find his
own asylum. Certainly not in this crib in this apartment
with the people who take this photograph.

LEFT TO RIGHT: David, Pat, and Mom (1951)

1951 . . . gingerly

She only has fingers for us,
no arms, no breasts, no cheeks.

We are toxin to be handled
gingerly for fear of infection, for
fear of disruption, for
fear.

David, she made jokes, all through
the rest of our lives, about how she
would put you in the front room and
it would take you an hour to crawl to
the kitchen where, with me (in a chair?
along the wall?), she did her tasks with
efficiency and speed. (She would brag,
all through the rest of our lives, how she
could take a bath in five minutes.) She
needed the lines she drew around her life
and around us. We were dangerous territory.

LEFT TO RIGHT: David and Pat (1952)

1952 . . . galvanized

I don't want to think of you
at 18 months, chewing on
the metal end of a garden
hose with a look of close concentration
while I stand behind you
in a galvanized iron tub,
our swimming pool. You teased
at the puzzles of life and were
teased. You picked at the scab of
pain, ripping it off again and again to
get somewhere you didn't know and
never reached. It was the way you knew to stay
alive until the raw suffering filled you like
helium and you rose, a Macy's float, to hang
over your life until you cut the cord
and fell.

LEFT TO RIGHT: David, Mary Beth, and Pat (1952)

1952 . . . photographer

A photographer was paid to take this photograph
of the three of us, unsmiling. One-year-old
Mary Beth has been set down on the chairs at
an odd angle. David's shirt isn't buttoned, and
his face is unsure of what to feel — a look I saw
many times over the next six decades. I am
looking back, like a frontiersman, into the forest
from which we have just emerged and trying to
read signs.

Merry Christmas!

LEFT TO RIGHT: David and Pat (1953)

1953 . . . coats

Written on the back, in the
hand of our muted father:

"David + Patrick
wearing new coats
they got from their
Aunt Mary."

He does not write that
we look like miniature
rich people. Like diplomats — David
with his chin up like a Lilliputian
Churchill. We look like Soviet
generals. Like boys who belong
in these coats with their thick
belts and thick-button fronts
and fur-like collars.

Our younger brother Tim will
strike that Churchill pose often
in the future. It was a gambit to
stretch to be seen amid all the
lines and angles that constrained
him. Did he learn it from David?

I am an uncomfortable prince, knowing
I am not a prince.

Neither of us is who we look.
We will wear these coats rarely,
too easy to stain, and grow
out of them soon.

We were neither military nor statesmen.
We navigated the world in our own ways —
side glances for me, scheming an opening,
and, for David, blunt naïveté. The boy
was never sure of himself though he
looked that way on that day when our
father made the image of us before

the house on Leamington, on the
West Side of Chicago, describing
us in a record empty of emotion.

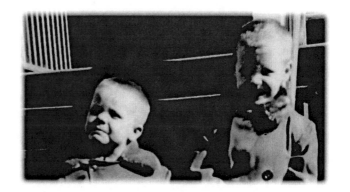

LEFT TO RIGHT: David, Mary Beth and Pat (1954)

1954 . . . circle

The four-year-old prophet made a
funny face to entertain his followers.

These three children in this moment
on the steps of a school in their clunky
shoes and tough-fabric clothes and
father-done haircut — they are arch-
angels of the Lord announcing the depth
of innocence in the world. Better than
archangels. They know pain and absence.
But they have found in this secret moment,
out in the open, a circle of three. Not a
one of them has a clue. They face life with
raw nerves. But they lean toward each other.

LEFT TO RIGHT: Pat, Eileen, David, and Mary Beth (1954)

1954 . . . innocent

The televisions are
too loud here in this glum
doctor's office where I
wait for Cathy to come
for her pre-op visit
with the knee replacement
surgeon. We've been through this
three other times, two for me
and one for Cathy, and
all with the result of
strong, new knees and carefree
walking, even running.

David died of his own
hand after his doctor
told him he needed four
operations on his
two shoulders and two hips —
this after the raw cruel
horror of surgery
on his back that left him
out of his mind for a
month, out of control, un-
protected. "I can't do
four more," he told me, hours
before he took the gun
and dragged himself to the
backyard so as not to
leave a mess.

We, four, are at the top
of some steps — notice the
railing — Eileen, in a
toy buggy; Mary Beth and
David; and I with a
half-smile on my face, no
delight there, hard to read.
What did I think was coming?

Eileen and Mary Beth

are caught in some halfway
place. David, you too look
in-between, your large head
thick with thought and feeling.
The neckline of your pa-
jama top is askew
as is mine. My smile may
be a cringe. Or maybe
a hope. Your lack of a
smile is sorrowful, as
if you were — as if you
knew you were — innocence
led blameless and confused
to the slaughter.

David (1955)

We wore
the cape
of a super-
hero but
knew it
was a
sham as
we were
shams, but
aching to
know what
to do
and who
to be.

The sun
was a
taunt. There
was night
and there
was day,
but we
could not
get to
our own
light.

LEFT TO RIGHT: David and Pat (1955)

1955 . . . Christmas

David smiles wide
under a jungle explorer helmet.
So do I. Our smiles toothy and
without restraint, as if there
will be no future.

We wear fake buckskin
with regimented fake leather fringe
that came with the fake coonskin caps
we wore like the TV star.
We could not believe our luck.

The Davy Crockett outfits and — there
must have been a sale — the jungle
explorer getups, simpler, just a
jungle explorer helmet and
a jungle explorer rifle
to kill big game.
We mixed and
matched.

Not knowing
the helmets
were called
pith helmets.

Not knowing
the small
explosion
that would
come sixty
years later
when the
hammer
struck
the
firing
pin.

LEFT TO RIGHT: Pat, Mary Beth, and David (1955)

1955 . . . naked

We three were born
one-two-three
in 25 months.

Mary Beth and I are swinging
on the backyard swing set,
high, smooth, bright in morning light,
singing songs we know at the top of our voices
and we might join hands,
lift off from the swings and fly out into
the clouds and all the way
to heaven where
Father God and
Mother Mary
will become
our doting parents.

David, that night
was filled with pain
and despair, and you
were as fragile as the
baby you had been
when first the cracks
were caused.

We were naked
and innocent
together.

LEFT TO RIGHT: David and Pat (1955)

1955 . . . pajamas

Straight we stand,
pajamas soft, warm —
it must be Christmas.
The camera is out.

I want to weep and weep and weep
for you, David,
and for me

We went from here further into the pain.
You closed up like a runner to protect the ball,
your head down, bulling ahead.

There was nobility in your charge at the world
and blindness.

We are only boys still
though you are ashes in an urn
and I carry years like demons and archangels on my shoulders.

Remember the smell of the incense at Mass?
You are incense now filling my church
with strange aromas.

> *(Priest) Introibo ad altare Dei.*
> *(Altar boys) Ad Deum qui laetificat juventutem meam.*

On our knees,
bent double
at the bottom of the steps to the altar,
mumbling — rushing, guessing, unsure,
uncertain, going into the jungle because
it had to be done —
in a language
not our own

> *I will go to the altar of God.*
> *To God, Who gives joy to my youth.*

Remember the burning coal on which
we dribbled small stones of incense?

The angel flew down and, with his
hand, gently lifted a burning coal from
the blaze and touched the coal to the
lips of Isaiah, and his sins were forgiven.

Prophesy, prophesy. Prophesy.

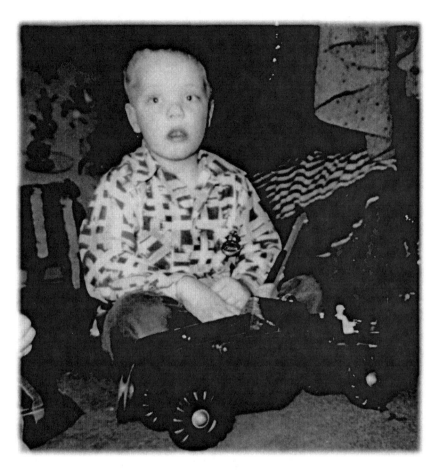

David, age four (1955)

1955 . . . stare

I know that
distant stare
to a world
not here.

LEFT TO RIGHT: David and Pat (1956)

1956 . . . corner

Easter, on Leamington. I
could go to that corner
today. It would take me an
hour. I could stand in the
spot where Dad took the
photo and see the two-flat kitty-
corner with its dark bricks. The
same trees might still be there. I
am sure the right-angle of the
curb is there, the two lines of
concrete that, with the two lines
of sidewalk, form the rectangle
of grass behind us. I could find
the spot where we stood in our
new clothes — me, one bent-
knee, an awkward stance, an
awkward feel to my skin; you
with arms straight at your side,
a smile on your face, as I have,
maybe a grin, maybe only the
result of the noon sun in the eyes.

I can go to that corner to see the
street and the sidewalk and grass
and building and feel again the
noon sun and my own awkwardness
and never find you.

LEFT TO RIGHT: Pat, David, and Tim (1956)

1956 . . . center

Tim, you were always a
comedian. You wore humor
like a bulletproof vest. You
are shouting here, or singing
here, or crowing here to the
moon.

In our Dad-buzz haircuts, our
thick fabric pants, our long-sleeve
shirts, we are three, laughing, smiling.
We are brothers in this moment together,
but the laughter
won't be strong enough
to keep us together because
Mom and Dad know they have to
keep us apart to keep their place at
the center of our hearts, no matter what we want.

LEFT TO RIGHT: David and Pat (1956)

1956 . . . son

Gabriel, blow!
Gabriel, blow!
Gabriel, blow!
Gabriel, blow!
Gabriel, blow!
Gabriel, blow!
Gabriel, blow!
Gabriel, blow!

Wake up, Lord of Lords!
Look at your son who has suffered on the altar of life.
Look! Look! Look!

Take him into your arms in an embrace he never found on this sorrowful earth.

Take him home. Be a fucking father to him.

Top to bottom: Pat and David (1956)

1956 . . . snow

Same pose — righty,
lefty — same shovel
stance, same
sun on boy faces,
same grin at the blood
filling muscle and heart and
head, same proud work.

We were seven and
nearly six.

Same tight bundled
bodies in the same
sharp, clear-clear
cold — boots, jeans,
jacket. David in a
hood. Me in a flapped cap.

Snow over the
white world, thin — over
the cars, the street, the
grass, the sidewalk along
the apartment building where,
later, a man died alone, and
David chinneyed up to look in
the first floor window to
see what had come
and would.

LEFT TO RIGHT: Mary Beth, Pat, and David (1956)

Come here, children, under my six-year-old wings.
I will protect you. I have taken the Lord into my gut.
I am strong. I am tall. I am your brother.

I failed.

Even then, I knew my own empty, tinny, echoing
spaces and found more later and, later, more. I
was struggling to stay upright. I was not up to being
alive. But I was. I went on my journey in the
wilderness. I left you both behind and all the
others. I needed my wings to protect my face
against the random slaps and jabs. I never told
you that, on a bus, a kid getting off punched me
in the face. Maybe on a dare. I didn't know him. I
was about this age, maybe a year or two older. On
the same field trip or another, a man behind me
rubbed himself against my butt in line to get into the
zoo or something. What could I say? I was being used
and was trapped in the open. You both had your
slaps and jabs and punches and rubs. You both were
alone. We are born alone. We die alone. David, you
know that. You made your own way to that moment,
and I failed you as I have failed myself all through life,
just as I have risen to life with joy despite the pain,
with hope despite the emptiness. I am a fool to believe.
You said that enough times, David. I was a fool to
think that my six-year-old wings could protect you
and Mary Beth. But I yearned to protect you as I had
no protection.

TOP TO BOTTOM: David and Pat (1960)

1960 . . . cap

I hated that hat like Dad's, and that
jacket — all jackets — I buried my
fists in the pockets — Dad made the
joke to Mom at the dinner table as I
stood there that I looked like a woman
with deep-drooping breasts.

Jesus! Jesus! Jesus!

You had a smile for life, wide, here filled with gaps,
a wide grin, a joy that was always there amid your
pain and fire and sad, sad choices. I wish you knew my
guards. I wish I knew how to reach past them to you
before you left. I wish I could see your smile again.

LEFT TO RIGHT: David, Mom, and Pat (1967)

1967 . . . tall

See the chains
that hold these
two tall boys
to that short
woman who
smiles out of
her fear and
dread, but sure
of the linked
locks she has
not only on
these two. Eleven
others are held
and one yet to
be born, to sit
around her sad
altar of need
— Oh, how we knew
and did not know
her pain and our
pain and the pain
of the world. We
are born to die.

I want to scream here
on this bench in New
York where strollers and
pigeons mingle before
the Met where artists, long
beyond pain, are cradled
in their wonder and
suffering, in their
suffering and
confused yearning
as we yearned for
what we did not
know, as she yearned
for what she knew not.

LEFT TO RIGHT: Pat and David (2002)

When did you learn to put your arm over my shoulder?

It was one of those years when you were always angry with me.

Mom was dead. Dad was waiting to die. We were orphans. As we had always been.

You were so filled with rage to get me to see you.

I was a rock on which your wave broke.

I was battered. You were broken.

But, at this moment before this camera, you put your arm over my shoulder in friendship.

We were brothers again in our fancy coats and pith helmets and raw happy grins even as she was encasing each of us in a carapace from which we fought, each alone, to escape.

We were brothers and never figured out what that meant.

LEFT TO RIGHT: David and Pat (2014)

We joked at the family Christmas party who would be the first among us fourteen to die.

You leaned to me with your eyes that way you had, a sideways glance, looking to me like we were conspirators.

You whispered to me thin humor as I sat leaning forward, head bent, like a priest hearing you confess.

I was on guard still to your easy spark of angry debate, but you here were my childhood brother ally.

I fear you looked to me for too much that I would not give, fearing to slide back into Mom's abyss.

We were skin of skin, blood of blood. We were the same raw slash.

De Profundis

Fire

My fires were banked, walled, held.
Yours were always ready to explode

until your last months when, in your
pain and fragility, you found some-
thing. Your flames sank. You no
longer frightened me as you had
with your aching demand that I
say yes to your complicated answer
to the simple, sad life we have to
lead once we are born.

You were born and found the same
empty space that greeted me.

Oh, David. I wish I had known how
to hug you. We never learned hugs
or listening, and our lessons were
hard, even as we tried to tell our-
selves that they were for our own
good.

Oh, David. Those last ten days of
pain were another hell for you. New
fires to lick your skin and shake your
lost strength.

We were fragile boys. You stuttered
and I wet the bed. I fell from
the top bunk and split my lip open. I
gave no cry for help. I crawled into
bed with you.

David Reardon (1951-2015)

You were there, David, with me.
I was there with you.

We were drawn together and pushed apart
by circumstances,
our souls,
our yearnings,
ignorant luck and
fatal choice.

Now you have left without me.
I am left without you.

"And I learned a lesson"

You heard
Dad's hard
words as
lessons
to make
the hammer
blows
seem
softer.

For a dollar

White t-shirt,
gray cotton work pants,
you were only nine but a
neighborhood boy like Roy
Eid and G.J. Lejeune.
Older they were
and stalwart as
you wished to be.

The odd cement structure
at the corner of the back
fence was for garbage
— three feet tall, two
and a half feet wide
and deep, next to the
crabapple tree. You
ate a crabapple because
it was an apple, though
small and bug-spotted.

There was a lid on top
for garbage to be dropped
in, and a lid in front at the
base where it met the alley
for garbagemen to shovel
the rubbish out.

In the home movie,
you take the metal
lid on top and lift it
and drop it as if it is
slimy. I think you
thought you would
climb into the empty
cement box, and maybe
find a home.

Fourteen years later,
thirteen miles away in
another part of Chicago,

at another family home fence,
you take my dare and
jump over the cyclone
metal without touching
it and win my dollar.

You were young, then, and
alive.

Broke

David slammed at Mom's goddess boulder
and Dad's black obelisk and
broke his hands

and broke his heart

and told himself —
and was told —
he was
wrong.

Loop

That Sunday,
you go the Loop
with your friends
on the el. They
ditch you and
come back to the
neighborhood.

You're maybe
eleven.

All you have to
do is to take the
quarter in your
pocket, get on
the el and you'll
be back at Lake
and Laramie in a
snap.

You get on the wrong el.

When you figure this
out, you walk back
downtown under the
el, find Lake Street
and start walking
west.

Seven miles.

Mom and Dad have the
cops and everyone looking,
and you walk in the back
door.

We were trained.

"I wasn't lost," you
said. "I knew where

I was."

We didn't know help could be
gotten.

Lesson

David died
because he learned a lesson
from Dad and Mom
that he was wrong and unworthy
and worthy only to kneel
with the rest at their altar
and sing Hosannas. Alleluia.

Am I unfair?

Did she laugh at David as a fat baby?
Did she egg him on
with arguments he could never win?
Did she hug him?

Did he take David under
his wing and tell the boy
he saw the sap and pride
and steel in his young soul?

Did he slap David down again and again?
For wanting other clothes?
For sneaking a teenage beer?
For yearning to be seen?

Did she put her hand gently to David's soft cheek?

Why do you think he stuttered?

God,
David made many sad choices.
David was blind and he was blinded.

He saw no way to escape their circle of fear.
He was a prisoner of their fear, as they were.

But they died in their beds.

A lament

Weep, Virgin Mother. Weep, you
other Marys. Weep, John at the
cross foot where the blood and
sweat dripped, where the
muscles of the Man ached,
cramped, tore and, eventually,
sagged the ghost away, the
soul off to open the gates of some
wayside hell between here and the
empty white. The terra cotta
scene by one of the Della Robbias
on the dark wall of the Gardner Museum
shines in the gloom, a "Lamentation." In His
dying, we are born. We are
seeds, blooming in the
hurricane, and withering
away to soil. My soil magnifies
the Lord, and my spirit within
me shouts against the vast empty
white, like Job, and then I am left,
like Job, in the silence to
endure.

Three hundred and sixteen days later

The man is preaching to a table
of Bible study men and women in
the McDonald's on 56th Street
at Eighth Avenue in New York City,
and I wish his Lord Jesus
was the on-off switch he describes.

You rejected the light-switch Jesus
you couldn't find.

I heard Jesus in the music.
I smelled Jesus in the incense and shit.
I felt Jesus in the Alleluia spaces
of the churches and the city. I
walk the streets of Manhattan and
Chicago and I touch Jesus in the red
bricks of apartment buildings
and see Jesus in the golden afternoon
sun on the apartment building wall.

The lady at the Bible study table
is praying to the Lord for a son with
sinus illness and throat illness,
for blessing from the crown
of his head to the soles of his feet.
Your pain was to the soul.

Could you have walked these streets
with me? Could I have given them
to you? Even thought to have given?

You were in the furnace and
the flames ate you.

You were in the lion's den and
devoured.

She is praying for her brother now.

I pray God hugged you in heaven

who did not hug you on earth.

Oh, David. I failed you and
you failed me. We failed our-
selves. And made our way.

She is blessing McDonald's now.

I went through the jungle and
found the jungle. You went into the
jungle and lost your way.

We can only fail. We
can only hope. We struggle or
don't.

I affirm.
You took control
and brought the end.

You were blinded by the
religion of the boulder
goddess who was an
eggshell skin over a
bag of fear. She taunted you
out of her dread. Her shell
was too thin to let you in but you
could not see. I only saw the need to
run.

Fault

Strong child,
stubborn parent
fearful, fragile,
needing to lock
the child away
from what might bring
more strength, needing
to turn the child —
like flower to
the blinding sun —
to the parent,
at the center
of all where strength
is fault and fear
is the only
power.

Three hundred and thirty days later

With a change in the weather,
my joints ache and I find
sorrow is the air I breathe

even as a silvery joy
flows beneath my skin

and I hold both
like a chalice of wine and blood
and lift to my lips
to drink.

Name

She called you David Michael.
You were only her son, not her husband.
You weren't David Joseph, her Dave.

For me, you are David.

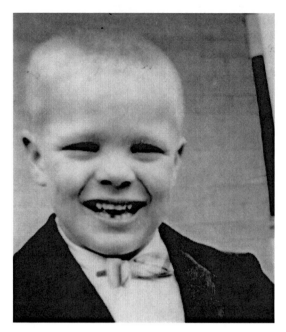

David (1957)

Able to choose

Let me honor your courage
to take your life. Oh, David,
why could you not find the
bravery to break out of your
prison before that, the penitentiary
Dad and Mom erected to keep
them safe from your raw life?
They could not live outside the
prison they made for themselves
and for you. And, in the end,
you couldn't.

Oh, David, I flew. I protected
myself. Why didn't you take to
the wing and grow your hair long
and really say fuck you to the church
and to Mom and Dad and find the raw
ripe life that always eluded you.

I am walking to Evanston through a
cold autumn afternoon, and my nose
runs as if I am crying on this trail of
tears and it almost seems that I am.
But I'm not, of course. You know,
David, that we learned early that
crying did us no good.

Oh, David, you were victimized and
victimized yourself. You tried to be
your deep self inside the world they
made so you could not find your
depth. It warped you, and, damn it,
David, it warped me and the others.

Oh, David, you sought to be strong but
fell under their weight. The world
was so full, but you could never get to
it wearing their straitjacket. You thought
each book you read was right, had to be
right. She taught you there was only true

and false, right and wrong, and she was
the one who
decided.

Oh, David, I wish you could have heard
the music I heard. I wish you could have
risen up and out and beyond on the wings
of words and beauty and disturbing visions.
You could have. It could have happened.

Damn it, David. Why did I survive?

Our last talk,
hours before
the shot was
our most real.

I loved you in
that moment
as I love you
now as I have
loved you from
your birth. In
that moment, I
saw your depth,
and we stood
together, knowing
neither of us had
anything we could
do beyond what
we had been able
to choose.

Your smile was an
explosion.

Your death

Your death
tore me
open like
the baby
was coming
out.

A Canticle for Pat

Babe

If I had a Mama
who would see me.
If I had a Mama
who would hear my aching cry.

If I had a Mama
who had a soft touch along the skin of my face.
If I had a Mama
who had talk for me and eyes to look in my eyes.

If I had a Mama
who would hold me as
a heart of her heart, not a carton of shit.

If I had a Mama
who would not laugh at me.

Goddess boulder

In Boston,
at the MFA,
the faith, love and hope
of the Della Robbia family art,
glazed terra cotta, one hundred
and fifty years of saints and
Madonnas with their Baby Jesus,
the colors, five centuries old,
glow like the warmth
of living skin.

Then, with directions, I
to the basement gallery of Olmec art
to confront the huge squat
crushing ugly boulder
goddess that is shown in
the museum guide and know
it is the weight and
threat of my mother

and find, instead,
a life-size jade priest mask, turned
by fire from green to gray, delicate, deadly
attractive but not looming.
Not huge. Only maybe
pained. Seeming as much
victim as butcher, except, of course,
to the
one
to be
sacrificed.

In the kitchen,
she sang with Frank
Sinatra about a surrey
with fringe, and, in that
moment, she was the most
beautiful girl in the world.

Mother

You
felt my words a threat
so claimed the talent as yours
though you never read them or
not enough of them to react to what
they were or meant. You did not want
to see me in the words. You wanted words
of praise for you. You feared the raw and ripped
and electric and apprehension in the words and
the edge of crazy and beyond and picked nits
as you nitpicked the ballet dancers on
TV, peering close, looking always
for the flaw, for the mis-move.
It took me long to know that
failure isn't evil. Evil is
curling up and waiting
decades to officially
die.

Father

You took no joy from me
and not from anything else,
only your wife, our mother.

When you entered the house,
you pulled her close,
bent her over,
and kissed her deeply.

We did not exist.

Lungs

You clung to each other
and looked only into
each other's eyes and
sank ever deeper away
from the frightening
air and sun and wind
and weather above the
surface. You feared at
any moment your lungs
filling with breath.

Drive away

In confession
the priest said in an
angry voice that the way
to drive away temptation
was to think of a woman
shitting.

The boy had only touched
himself.

At the door

A bike without brakes?
A rider who never learned to use them?

A frail neighbor woman on the sidewalk, Mrs. Murtaugh,
with a trace of blood near her glasses.
A boy back upstairs trying to forget.

A policeman at the door.

Providence

The nun said:
Pray for your sins.
Be watchful.
The Lord is like electricity.
Make no false move.

A watery echo

The home movies
show how red my
skin got from the
sun that day and
many other
days at the kids
blue-bottom pool
at Columbus
Park. We were all
so pale, Irish,
red and blond hair,
and deep sunburn,
on which we put
cool Noxema.

The odd-shape dark
spot the nice young
doctor found on
my back forty
years later was
a hot echo:
melanoma.

Never read

Never read,
the book I won
at some meeting
of some eighth-grade boys
in a hall in downtown Chicago
— *Drop the Dagger!* —
(and a scholarship)
nudged me to
the seminary
that was the
first step on the
road to here.

I ache
for that boy
who was
running
full tilt
to me,

to sorrow
and elation.

Then

At Christmas,
there is me.

Then David.
Then Mary Beth.
Then Eileen.
Then Tim.
Then John.
Then Rosemary.
Then Laura.
Then Marie.
Then Kathy.
Then Teri.
Then Geri.
Then Jeanne.
Then Rita.

Every baby is the Baby Jesus.

One Christmas morning sixty years ago,
Mary Beth suddenly grabs
a metal fire truck from my grasp,
leaving me with a short, thin slice of blood on my palm.
Nothing to be done but find, unnoticed,
a Band Aid in the bathroom.

We are the brothers and sisters of Baby Jesus.

God hides,
like a
small
child,
for
fun.

Grandma

The showers have turned to drizzle.
Drops fall heavily now
from the black limbs of a bare tree
in the glare of the street light.
She is tired.
She is worse today.
Some talk
and some smoke
and some run for office.
She has laughed at the scandals of others.

She is worse today.
She is close to shore.
She has baked no bread in seven years.
She has not gone to Mass in two years.
She has not smoked in a year.
Her sewing has become knitting.
She no longer watches television.
She is tired.

The Commission members
discuss the image of women in advertisements.
They argue strategies.
They choose sides.
She used to pawn her wedding ring
and redeem it when the check came in.
She is worse today.

She has been petty in old age.
She has betrayed and aggravated.
She has found small pleasures
inflicting small wounds.
She is tired.

She has lived to see
the children of her children's children
and has taken life from their young lives.
Her heart is failing.
She cannot hear well.
She walks on the arm of a grandson.

The rain has stopped
and the night is silent
but for the single car
moving quietly down the street.

She is a child now
afraid of growing up.
She is tired.

She is worse today.

Altar

I offer the purple sash
and the white surplice.

I offer the cold mornings
when snow crunched
and the church was dark
and silent
and an old man
came down the aisle.

I offer the cruets,
and the words at the foot of the altar,
and the priest, heavy with vestments.

    Introibo ad altare Dei.

I offer the bells and the cross,
and incense sprinkled on coals.

I offer
the long white tapers
and the flames.

    Ad Deum qui laetificat juventutem meam.

Magnificat

My soul magnifies the Lord and my spirit
rejoices in God my Savior. — Luke 1: 46-55

I am God's magnifying glass.
My heart thrills.

I am a worm and no man, but blessed.

God of might, God of holiness, God of mercy.
The proud scattered. The high brought low,
sent empty away.

The poor
on the cliff at the chasm,
looking down at the wealthy,
arms extended above the
flames.

The poor,
fed.

July 10, 1981

On this porch, on this cool
summer day, when the moon
is benign in afternoon sky,
when birds sing from wire to
wire, I have no argument.
This may be the milk-and-
honey time, the fulcrum,
the equator. I may be on
my way down or past or
into. This will change, and
I will change, and the wood
of this porch will rot. The
birds will die, and I will die,
and new leaves will grow
under other summer suns.
I have no argument.

Standing before Turner's
"Fall of the Rhine at Schaffhausen"
in the Boston Museum of Fine Arts

The pounding crush of the falling
Rhine waters has no end unlike
these tiny foreground
figures who reach and
stretch to accomplish their
small tasks, muscles straining,
reaching, stretching,
yearning.

A few feet from this Turner is one of Manet's
oils of the shooting squad execution of
fake Mexican Emperor Maximilian, a
fool if there ever was one, but
aren't we all
fools who
end in the
vague smoke
awaiting the
coup de grâce?

What, though, is the alternative?
The urgency, as Brooks says, is in
the blooming
amid the noise
and power
of the flood.

We are all, victims and butchers, crushed
by the same cataract,
slain by the same
bullet. You and me and
David.

Haitian cabbie

You born
You sign to die — hah!
It contract
you sign — hah!

If you with God
you spirit leaves.
You talk to God.
You body's on the floor.

You have an angel to escort you.
Escort, you know.
The Devil all around,
you need escort.

If you are with the Devil
you spirit just stays there.

You believe in God
you a light.

It is hard.

The endless white around the corner

I know it comes, not when.

I am running to it, racing, straining,
through the brittle leaves, the boggy mulch,
deeply breathing in and out,
alive to the breathing, to the muscles, to my sweat,
to the rhythm, to the light —
so much light.

I walk the cemetery.

I study the newsreel of the King's coronation.
He is gone. So are they all,
gone, decayed, disappeared.

I am Lincoln in the moment of the bullet's entry.

I am books unread. Books not written.

I am the red-brick apartment building in the rising sun,
more beautiful
than Solomon
in all his glory.
I am the deep green grass of a child's lullaby,
a dumb green field.

I am Earth from space,
the stars.

I am a wildflower downtown in a concrete curb.
I am a sound, echoing.

I am in the boat with others
alone.

Follow like children

Dirt flies buzz his face.
They lick sweat in the bold wounds
of his head and hands and feet.
They crawl up the ripped and torn terrain
of his back.
They are acolytes to his sacrifice,
adding their fly's weight.

They will continue
until mid-afternoon.
He will die,
be taken down and carried to the cave.
They will follow like children,
running in and out to be forgotten and caught in the
rolling of the stone.

They will zigzag to insane corners,
looking for escape
and will find none.

After three days,
they will be lying down
to die
as the movement of sheets
takes form.

The bullet enters Lincoln's skull

He dreamed
and saw her under the tree
in the pink dress her mother hated.

He felt a small hand in his
in the darkness
and wanted to escort the boy.

He saw the sun of that afternoon on the circuit
when the horse was lame
and he had a headache.

He heard the voices of the hecklers
for the first time clearly.

He saw the burned city
and the white city
and the prairie town Capitol.

He smelled the market stores
along the river
and the fish there
for purchase.

He saw his father by the woodblock
with an axe in his hands
and the body of an animal at his feet.

He tasted blood.

What else?

I walk through thick curtains of liquid sorrow
because what else is there to do?

This watery drag on my muscles and skin
tides with seasons and years.

In 1981, I was a drowned man walking,
struggling without sight to
find purchase in the fluid to
climb up and out to
somewhere I could not imagine.

David, you knew this
watery knowledge and ignorance.

Why did I find air?
Why did you not?

Now I am drowned again, seeking
a handhold because, David, you knew
what else there was to do.

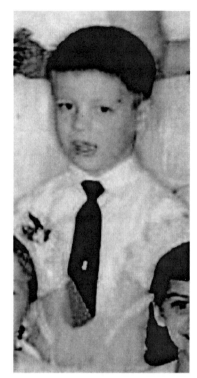

Pat (1956)

A canticle for Pat

He looks out from the cave of his skull.

His lip is swollen from a top bunk fall.

His hair is cut by his father.

His First Communion shirt,
his First Communion tie
draw attention.

He is in the cavern of the church,
in the rows of children, alone.

He soars up,
up the gold spire atop the altar,
up the stained glass windows,
blue with sparks of red, green, white, gold,
up the mighty organ chords,
up the Host to heaven.

The brown wood of the pews
is new-turned soil.

He is suspended.

He waits.

Ordinary time

In the sacred church space,
during a Mass in Ordinary Time,
I am visited by a vision, and each
of the stained glass windows
tells the story of my life,
and in each one is a
crucifixion and a
flower pushing up
through soil and up
and out and up to
reach up and out and
open to the battering
wind and the bee and
the blessing of sun
and, then, the
snow.

We are all Elijah on the mountain

The still, small voice
is still
an itch in the corner
of the skull,
a catch of breath,
a comma, a hesitancy,
a heartbeat,
a hush,
a scratching at the edge,
a bloom in the storm,
a sideways glimpse,
small
as
a
spirit.

About the Author

Patrick T. Reardon is a Chicagoan, born and bred. He is the author of seven previous books, including *Faith Stripped to Its Essence: A Discordant Pilgrimage through Shusaku Endo's Silence.* Reardon worked for thirty-two years as a reporter with the *Chicago Tribune*, specializing in urban affairs, and is now writing a book about the untold story of the impact of the elevated railroad Loop on the stability and development of Chicago. His essays have appeared frequently in American and European publications, including the *Chicago Tribune, Chicago Sun-Times, Crain's Chicago Business, National Catholic Reporter, Illinois Heritage, Reality,* and *U.S. Catholic*. His book reviews have twice won the Peter Lisagor Award for arts criticism. He has lectured on Chicago history at the Chicago History Museum.

CPSIA information can be obtained
at www.ICGtesting.com
Printed in the USA
LVOW10s1943280417

532583LV00014B/277/P